Finding Happy

First published in India by HarperCollins *Children's Books* 2025
An imprint of HarperCollins *Publishers*
HarperCollins *Publishers* India, Cyber City, Building 10-A,
Gurugram, Haryana-122002, India
www.harpercollins.co.in

2 4 6 8 10 9 7 5 3 1

Text © Gulshan Advani 2025
Illustrations © HarperCollins *Publishers* India and Suvidha Mistry 2025

P-ISBN: 978-93-6989-314-0
E-ISBN: 978-93-6989-387-4

Gulshan Advani asserts the moral right
to be identified as the author of this work.

This is a work of fiction and all characters and incidents described
in this book are the product of the author's imagination.
Any resemblance to actual persons, living or dead, is entirely coincidental.

All rights reserved. No part of this publication may be reproduced, stored in a retrieval system, or transmitted, in any form or by any means, electronic, mechanical, photocopying, recording or otherwise, without the prior permission of the publishers.

Without limiting the exclusive rights of any author, contributor or the publisher of this publication, any unauthorized use of this publication to train generative artificial intelligence (AI) technologies is expressly prohibited. HarperCollins also exercise their rights under Article 4(3) of the Digital Single Market Directive 2019/790 and expressly reserve this publication from the text and data-mining exception.

Cover design and art by Suvidha Mistry
Inside illustrations by Suvidha Mistry

Typeset in 16/25 Alga at
HarperCollins *Publishers* India

Printed and bound at
Nutech Print Services - India

This book is printed on FSC® certified paper
which ensures responsible forest management.

HarperCollins Publishers, Macken House, 39/40 Mayor Street Upper, Dublin 1,
D01 C9W8, Ireland

Finding Happy

Gulshan Advani

Illustrated by
Suvidha Mistry

HarperCollins
Children's Books

Advance Praise for 'Finding Happy'

"A story about happiness, fun and joy that somehow is something that we all need right now... simply told but strongly put."

KAJOL DEVGAN
actor

"Rare is the book that has the sweet innocence of a child and the calm wisdom of an old person. *Finding Happy* is one such. It's a book that will make you smile as you read through it, and you will put it down with a thought to ponder over. Do read it."

AMISH TRIPATHI
author

To my biggest inspiration Agastya.

Thank you for letting me see the world through your rainbow-tinted lens.

On a faraway island in the middle of the sea,
There lived a little boy whose name was Gusty.
He had a skippy walk and long wavy hair,
A mischievous grin and a cheeky stare!

He woke up one morning, determined as can be.
Today he would be happy, he made a decree.
He knocked on doors, asking all his friends,
"Do you know how to be happy, on all days, not just weekends?"

Each scratched their chin and shook their head,
For none of them knew, and it filled them with dread.
It was indeed a very big question.
It made them think. It caught their attention.

"I have a suggestion," said his sister, Bella,
"Ask old wise man Kikoo. He's a smart fella!
He sits under the Banyan Tree up on the hill."
The idea was genius – it was simply brill!

Off he went, as brave as can be,
Past the village, full of glee.
The grass tickled him, making him giggle,
He danced, he bounced, he did a little jiggle!

*But wait, he hadn't got time for this,
He must find the wise man, he must be happy.*

He walked by the river, towards the hill,
Jumping over a tree trunk took some skill!
Just then, he heard a peculiar sound,
Beautiful and musical, not usually found.

As he sneaked closer to take a peek,
He saw the world's cutest beak.
A bird as colourful as can be,
Sitting right there on a magnificent tree!

He smiled and stared, what a beautiful sound,
He wondered where it came from and where it was bound.
What adventures did it have under the sky?
What was its view from up so high?

But wait, he hadn't got time for this,
He must find the wise man, he must be happy.

He jumped from the tree and walked along,
Climbing up a hill where the rocks belong.
His hands started hurting, his tummy rumbled,
"I need to eat something now," it grumbled.

Just that moment, he saw a tree,
Filled with mangoes, it was meant to be!
He jumped up with joy and gobbled a bunch,
Eating them happily, enjoying every munch!

Grinning at his stroke of luck,
Finding such sweetness for his tuck.
He rested a moment under the shade,
Feeling so pleased with the discovery
he'd made.

But wait, he hadn't got time for this,
He must find the wise man, he must be happy.

Past the rocks lay a flat garden,
He saw a girl and begged her pardon.
"Could you point me to the Ancient Banyan Tree?
There's a wise man I need to see."

She gave him directions, asked him to play,
But he said, "No time!" and set off on his way.
As he turned the corner towards the cliff,
The wind blew past, and he got a whiff.

A flowery, sweet-smelling tree!
It was filled with jasmine, he noticed with glee.
Falling like snow as it danced in the breeze,
He laughed and twirled, then fell to his knees.

But wait, he hadn't got time for this,
He must find the wise man, he must be happy.

He climbed to the top, full of thrill,
He was there! He had made it! He couldn't stay still.
He was going to be happy now,
And this wise man would tell him how.

"Oh Mr. Wise Man, I've been searching for you,
Can you tell me how to be happy? What should I do?
I want to find joy and feel good every day,
Please help me, show me the way."

The wise man lifted his brows, touched his chin,
Staring at Gusty with a knowing grin.
"Why little man, don't you see?
Happiness isn't a place or a plea."

"Happiness is in small things, that's the key.
It's everywhere you look, it's actually free!
It's what you feel, smell, hear and touch every day,
It's the feeling inside you that tingles
in a magical way."

Little Gusty knew now what it took,
His journey was filled with happiness,
In the tickle of the grass...
In the smell of the jasmine...
In the taste of the mango...
In the songs of the bird...
He only had to stop and look!

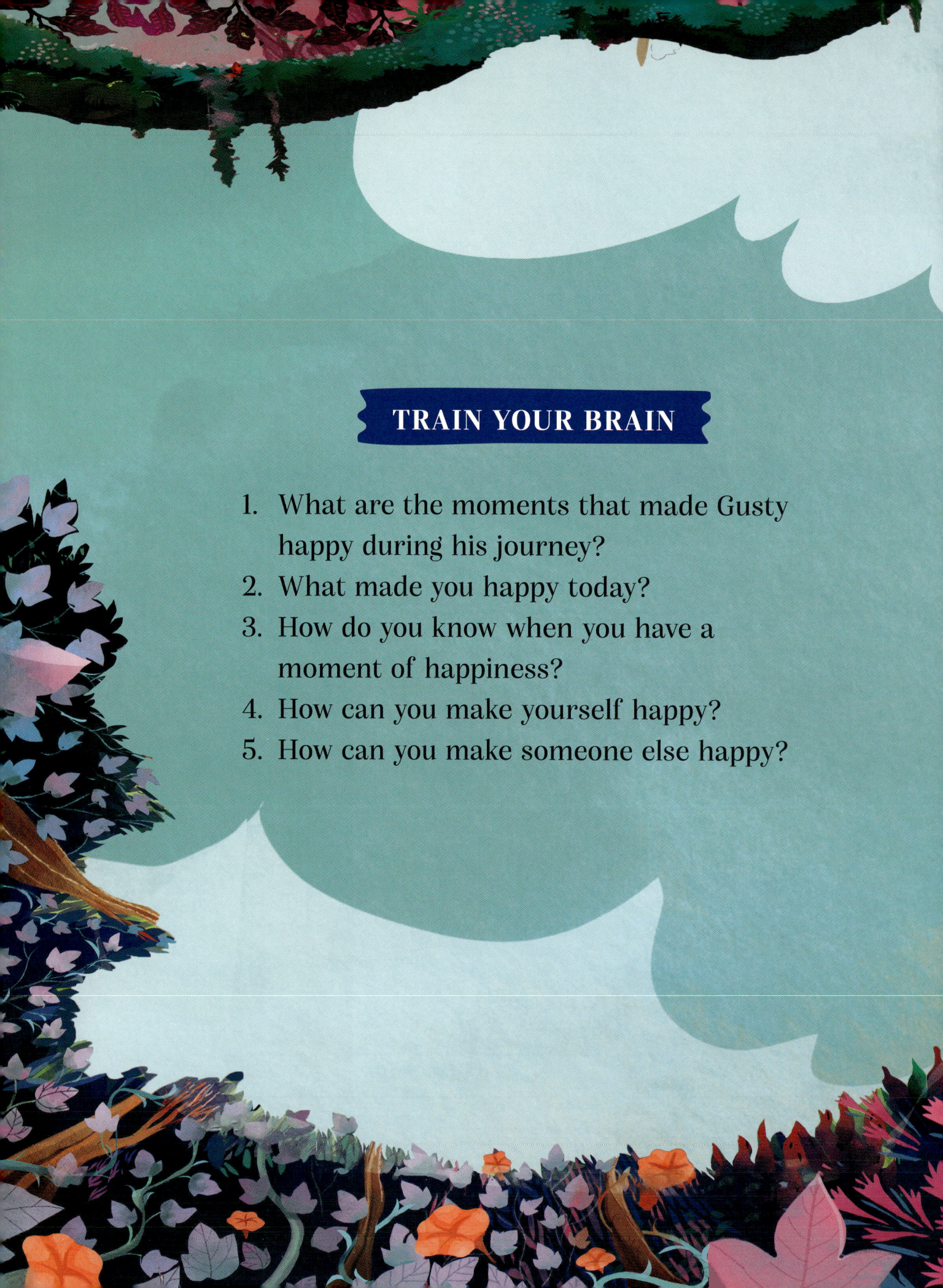

TRAIN YOUR BRAIN

1. What are the moments that made Gusty happy during his journey?
2. What made you happy today?
3. How do you know when you have a moment of happiness?
4. How can you make yourself happy?
5. How can you make someone else happy?

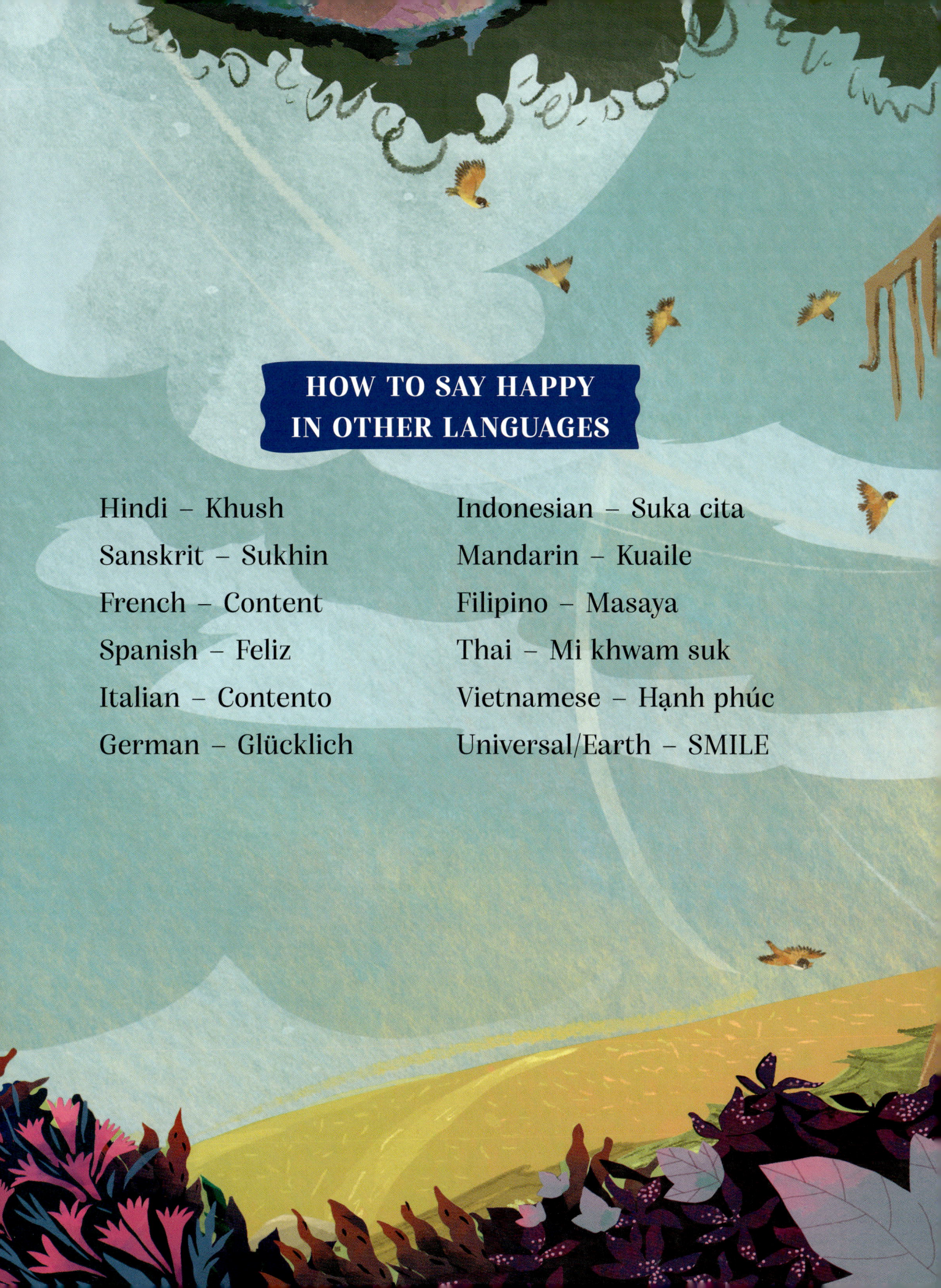

HOW TO SAY HAPPY IN OTHER LANGUAGES

Hindi – Khush
Sanskrit – Sukhin
French – Content
Spanish – Feliz
Italian – Contento
German – Glücklich

Indonesian – Suka cita
Mandarin – Kuaile
Filipino – Masaya
Thai – Mi khwam suk
Vietnamese – Hạnh phúc
Universal/Earth – SMILE

About the Author

GULSHAN RANDHAWA ADVANI has lived in Australia, India and Singapore. She has travelled the world, experienced countless adventures and met many remarkable people... all through books. In her quest to pass on her great love of reading to her son Agastya, she wrote her very first book, 'Finding Happy'. This is a story of a little man with a question, as he sets off on a quest to find the answers he knew all along. With this book and the others to follow she intends to tackle life's tricky topics in a light and entertaining way that children can relate to. With 20 years of marketing experience in publishing and fashion, this book was a surprising but not unexpected detour, born out of her own experiences as a mum trying to make the complex easy and the boring, fun!

About the Illustrator

SUVIDHA, an illustrator with years of experience with various publishing houses across India as well as multimedia and advertising agencies, felt her universe of imagination explode when she first illustrated for a children's book. This led her to many more books and several awards including the 'Publishing Next' in 2019 and a special honour by the Association of Writers and Illustrators for Children. She has participated in the Nambook010, International Children's Book Festival, Korea 2010. Her works have been exhibited in Korea and Bratislava.
An avid nature lover, she loves long journeys that gift her new ideas and dazzling memories. She revels in her terrace garden and has also been honoured for her design and development work on community gardens in her neighbourhood.